HOW DID THAT GET TO MY TABLE?

ORANGE JUICE

BY PAM ROSENBERG

COMMUNITY CONNECTIONS

CHERRY LAKE Publishing

ORANGE JUICE

Published in the United States of America by Cherry Lake Publishing
Ann Arbor, Michigan
www.cherrylakepublishing.com

Content Adviser: Anuradha Prakash, PhD, Professor, Food Science,
Chapman University
Reading Adviser: Cecilia Minden-Cupp, PhD, Literacy Consultant

Photo Credits: Cover and page 1, ©Sergei Didyk, used under license from Shutterstock, Inc.;
page 5, ©Monkeybusinessimages/Dreamstime.com; page 7, ©Kcphotos/Dreamstime.com;
pages 9, 11, and 13, ©Jim West/Alamy; page 15, ©Cristiano Burmester/Alamy; page 17,
©fStop/Alamy; page 19, ©Ronald Karpilo/Alamy; page 21, ©Gamutstockimagespvtltd/
Dreamstime.com

LIBRARY OF CONGRESS CATALOGING-IN-PUBLICATION DATA
Rosenberg, Pam.
  How did that get to my table? Orange juice / by Pam Rosenberg.
    p. cm.—(Community connections)
  Includes index.
  ISBN-13: 978-1-60279-468-9
  ISBN-10: 1-60279-468-5
  1. Orange juice—Juvenile literature. I. Title. II. Series.
  TX558.O7R57 2009
  641.3'431—dc22   2008053268

Cherry Lake Publishing would like to acknowledge the
work of The Partnership for 21st Century Skills. Please
visit www.21stcenturyskills.org for more information.

CONTENTS

4 A Juicy Fruit

6 Oranges Grow in Groves

8 At the Factory

18 From the Factory to Your Table

22 Glossary

23 Find Out More

24 Index

24 About the Author

A JUICY FRUIT

You just got back from a long bike ride. It is hot outside, and you are thirsty. You open the refrigerator to get a cold drink. You take out a carton of orange juice and pour some in your glass. Then you start to wonder. Where does orange juice come from?

Orange juice is tasty and refreshing.

ORANGES GROW IN GROVES

Most oranges grow in orange groves. A grove is a group of trees growing close together. Pickers pull ripe oranges off the trees by hand. Then the oranges are sent to a factory to be made into juice.

Oranges grow in warm, sunny places.

AT THE FACTORY

What happens at the factory? The oranges are put on a **conveyor belt**. They are washed with soap and special brushes. Then the oranges are rinsed and dried.

Workers remove any unripe or spoiled oranges. Only the best oranges are used to make orange juice.

These oranges are being washed at a factory in Belize. Belize is a country in Central America.

How many oranges do you think it takes to make a small glass of juice? Make a guess. Ask your parents to buy a bag of oranges. Cut them in half and squeeze out the juice. Was your guess correct?

9

How is the juice removed from the oranges? Special machines extract juice from the oranges. The machines squeeze the juice out of the oranges. The orange juice is passed through a screen. The screen helps filter out any large pieces of orange or orange peel from the juice.

Machines are used to get the juice out of oranges at factories.

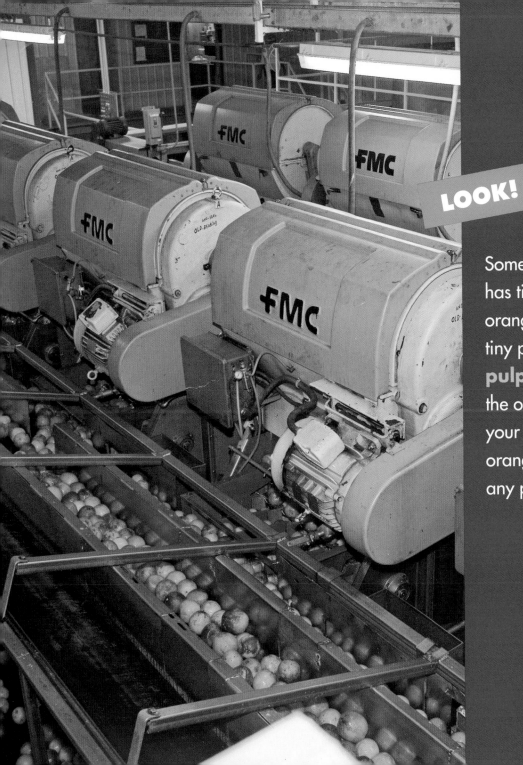

LOOK!

Some orange juice has tiny pieces of oranges in it. These tiny pieces are called **pulp**. Take a look at the orange juice in your glass. Does your orange juice have any pulp in it?

11

Next, the orange juice is heated. This removes much of the water. The remaining juice is called **concentrate**. Concentrate can be stored longer than fresh squeezed juice. Concentrate also costs less to store and ship. That's because it takes up less space. Juice companies often add water to the concentrate before **packaging** orange juice.

Can you see the orange juice flowing through these pipes? A worker is watching to be sure the machines are working correctly.

Concentrated orange juice is sometimes frozen. You can find it in your grocer's freezer case. You must add water to frozen juice before drinking it. How much water should you add? Usually, three juice cans of water are added. The juice is ready to drink after stirring.

Orange juice concentrate is stored in very large containers at factories.

Orange juice must be heated before it is put in cartons or bottles. Heating kills harmful **bacteria**. Killing bacteria with heat is called **pasteurization**. This helps keep juice safer and fresher longer.

After heating, the juice is put into containers. Filling machines pour the right amount of juice into each container. The containers are sealed and cooled.

Machines at factories can fill many bottles of juice in a day.

FROM THE FACTORY TO YOUR TABLE

Refrigerated trucks deliver orange juice to stores. Refrigerated store cases keep the orange juice cold until you buy it. Then it is up to you to make sure the juice stays cold until you drink it.

There are many kinds of juice to choose from at grocery stores.

THINK!

Some orange juice is prepared so it doesn't have to be kept cold. Can you think of one kind of orange juice container that doesn't have to be kept in your refrigerator? Hint: the containers usually come with a small straw attached to them.

19

Next time you are thirsty, pour yourself a cold glass of orange juice. Think about the journey from the orange grove to your table. Now drink and enjoy!

Time for a tasty glass of orange juice!

GLOSSARY

bacteria (bak-TIHR-ee-uh) very small living things that can spoil food or make people sick

concentrate (KON-sen-trayt) a food, such as orange juice, that is heated to remove water

conveyor belt (kuhn-VAY-ur BELT) a moving belt used to carry objects from one place to another in a factory

extract (ek-STRAKT) to remove something, such as squeezing oranges to remove their juice

groves (GROHVZ) groups of trees growing close together

packaging (PAK-ij-ing) putting a product in its container or wrapping

pasteurization (pass-chur-ih-ZAY-shuhn) a method of heating food to a temperature that kills harmful bacteria

pulp (PUHLP) the soft, fleshy pieces of a fruit or vegetable in juice

FIND OUT MORE

BOOKS

Mayo, Gretchen Will. *Orange Juice*. Milwaukee, WI: Weekly Reader Early Learning Library, 2004.

Snyder, Inez. *Oranges*. New York: Children's Press, 2004.

WEB SITES

Florida Department of Citrus
www.floridajuice.com/
Information about orange juice and links to games and activities

Fresh for Kids—Oranges!
www.freshforkids.com.au/fruit_pages/orange/orange.html
Learn more about different kinds of oranges and how they are grown at this Australian site

INDEX

bacteria, 16
bottles, 16

concentrate, 12, 14
containers, 4, 12,
    16, 19
conveyor belts, 8

extraction, 10

factories, 6, 8
filter screens, 10
frozen concentrate,
    14

heating, 12, 16

machines, 10, 16

orange groves, 6
oranges, 6, 8, 9,
    10, 11

pasteurization, 16
pickers, 6
pulp, 11

refrigerated trucks,
    18
refrigerators, 4, 18,
    19

stores, 18

trucks, 18

workers, 6, 8

ABOUT THE AUTHOR

Pam Rosenberg writes
and edits nonfiction
books for children.
She lives with her
family in Arlington
Heights, Illinois.
There is always
orange juice in
their refrigerator.